Nature is All Around Me

Numbers in Nature

by Jennifer Marino Walters

LOOK!
BOOKS™

Red Chair Press   Egremont, Massachusetts

Look! Books are produced and published by Red Chair Press:

Red Chair Press LLC   PO Box 333   South Egremont, MA 01258-0333

www.redchairpress.com

Publisher's Cataloging-In-Publication Data

Names: Marino Walters, Jennifer

Title: Numbers in nature / by Jennifer Marino Walters.

Description: Egremont, Massachusetts : Red Chair Press, [2018] | Series: Look! books : Nature is all around me | Interest age level: 004-007. | Includes Now You Know fact-boxes, a glossary, and resources for additional reading. | Includes index. | Summary: "The number of points on a starfish or on a snowflake, the number of moons in the night sky. Let's count how many surprises nature has all around us."--Provided by publisher.

Identifiers: ISBN 978-1-63440-298-9 (library hardcover) | ISBN 978-1-63440-354-2 (paperback) | ISBN 978-1-63440-302-3 (ebook)

Subjects: LCSH: Nature--Juvenile literature. | Counting--Juvenile literature. | CYAC: Nature. | Counting.

Classification: LCC QH48 .M37 2018 (print) | LCC QH48 (ebook) | DDC 508 [E]--dc23

LCCN 2017947522

Photo credits: Shutterstock except for the following; p. 5: iStock

Printed in the United States of America

0718 1P CGF18

Table of Contents

Look Up for Numbers So High

If you look closely, you'll see that the world is full of numbers. Let's count to 10 using things from **nature**. Here is **one** moon in the night sky. See the hawk flying high with its **two** wings spread wide.

Flowers have different numbers of **petals**. Many flowers, like these trilliums, have **three** petals.

Look All Around

Clovers with three leaves are **common**. But, four-leaf clovers are not common. If you find a four-leaf clover, keep it— it is said to bring good luck!

Most apples have **five** seed pockets that form a star shape. Each seed pocket can hold up to two seeds.

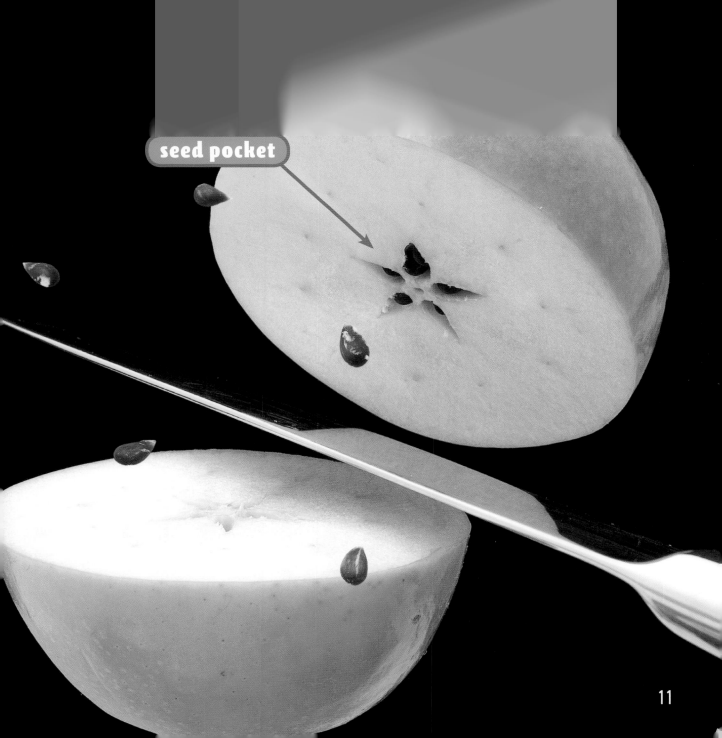

seed pocket

One of a Kind

Snowflakes come in many shapes and sizes. It is **rare** to find two that look alike. But, all snowflakes have **six** points.

Good to Know

The size of a snowflake depends on the number of ice crystals that connect together. Most flakes are made of about 200 crystals.

A ladybug's back can have many spots, few spots, or no spots. One type of ladybug has **seven** spots. Can you count them?

Good to Know

Some ladybugs, or ladybird beetles, even have stripes on their back. These colorful insects are helpful in the garden.

An octopus has **eight** arms, called tentacles. The octopus uses its arms to do things like walk across the ocean floor and catch **prey**.

Good to Know

An octopus is a type of animal without bones. It can squeeze in and out of tight spaces in the ocean.

tentacle

This Litter is Okay!

Humans usually have one baby at a time. But, some animals have many babies at once. Here is a **litter** of nine puppies! That's one busy mother!

Chimps are like humans in many ways. Like us, they have **ten** fingers and **ten** toes!

Good to Know

Chimpanzees and gorillas belong to the ape family. They can use tools and build things much like humans do.

Words to Keep

common: happening often

litter: the babies born to an animal at a single time

nature: the physical world and everything in it that is not made by people

petal: the colorful leaf of a flower

prey: an animal hunted by another animal for food

rare: not happening often

Learn More at the Library

(Check out these books to learn more.)

Adamson, Thomas K. and Heather. *2, 4, Skip Count Some More.* Capstone Press, 2012.

Salzman, Mary Elizabeth. *Know Your Numbers: Nature.* Abdo, 2014.

Index

About the Author

Jennifer Marino Walters likes exploring numbers in nature in Virginia with her three kids and one husband.